Cambridge English

Starters

AUTHENTIC EXAMINATION PAPERS

2

STUDENT'S BOOK

Cambridge University Press
www.cambridge.org/elt

Cambridge English Language Assessment
www.cambridgeenglish.org

Information on this title: www.cambridge.org/9781316636237

© Cambridge University Press and UCLES 2018

First published 2018

20 19 18 17 16 15 14 13 12

Printed in Malaysia by Vivar Printing

A catalogue record for this publication is available from the British Library

ISBN 978-1-316-63623-7 Student's Book
ISBN 978-1-316-63626-8 Answer Booklet
ISBN 978-1-316-63629-9 Audio CD

Cover illustration: (T) MashaStarus/iStock/Getty Images Plus; (B) adekvat/iStock/Getty Images Plus

Contents

Part 1

– 5 questions –

Listen and draw lines. There is one example.

Pat   Mark   Jill   Lucy

Hugo   Alice   Kim

Part 2
– 5 questions –

Read the question. Listen and write a name or a number.
There are two examples.

Examples

What is this robot's name?   .... Bill ....

How many robots has the boy got?   .... 11 ....

Questions

1 Which friend can the robot phone? ....

2 How many words can the robot say? ....

3 What is the name of the boy's cousin? ....

4 How many games can the robot play? ....

5 What is the cat's name? ....

Part 3
– 5 questions –

Listen and tick (✔) the box. There is one example.

Where is Alex now?

A ☐   B ✔   C ☐

1   What is Dad doing?

A ☐   B ☐   C ☐

2   Which is Anna's sister?

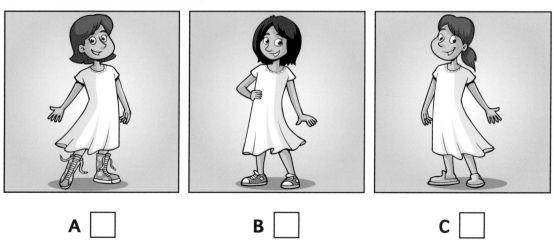

A ☐   B ☐   C ☐

3   What is in Sam's school bag?

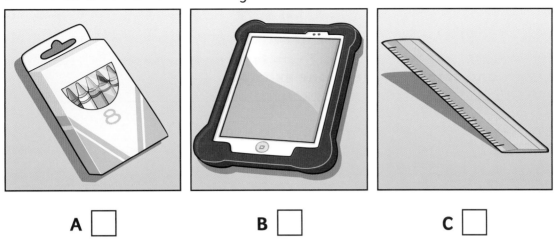

A ☐   B ☐   C ☐

4   Where are Grandpa's glasses?

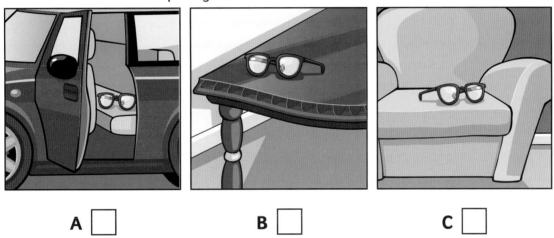

A ☐   B ☐   C ☐

5   What is May drawing?

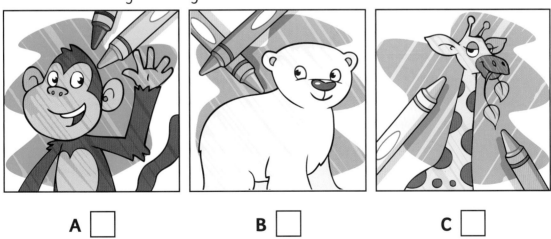

A ☐   B ☐   C ☐

Part 4

– 5 questions –

Listen and colour. There is one example.

Reading and Writing

Part 1

– 5 questions –

Look and read. Put a tick (✔) or a cross (✗) in the box.
There are two examples.

Examples

These are guitars.

This is a street.

Questions

1

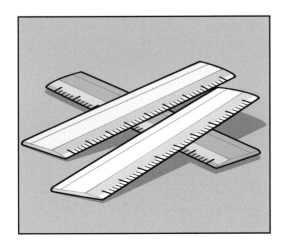

These are rulers.

2

This is a pie. ☐

3

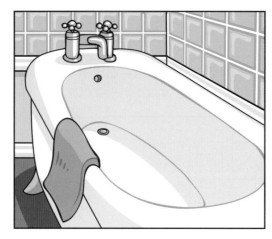

This is a bed. ☐

4

These are boards. ☐

5

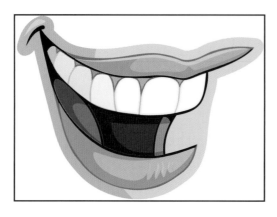

This is a mouth. ☐

Part 2

– 5 questions –

Look and read. Write yes or no.

Examples

The family is in their dining room. ....yes...............

The baby's balloon is blue. ....no...............

Questions

1 The mother has got some drinks. ....

2 One person is holding a camera. ....

3 You can see a doll on the table. ....

4 There is a tiger in the painting. ....

5 The door is closed. ....

Part 3
– 5 questions –

Look at the pictures. Look at the letters. Write the words.

Example

<u>h a t</u>

Questions

1

_ _ _ _ _

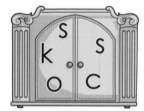

2

_ _ _ _ _

3

_ _ _ _ _

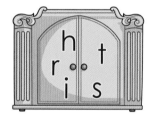

4

_ _ _ _ _

5

_ _ _ _ _ _

Part 4
– 5 questions –

Read this. Choose a word from the box. Write the correct word next to numbers 1–5. There is one example.

Mary's ducks

There are lots of animals on Mary's ....farm.... . There are some chickens,

and ducks and a **(1)** .... Mary likes the

ducks. The ducks are brown and white and they have big orange

(2) .... Mary gives the ducks

(3) .... in the morning. In the day, the ducks swim

in the **(4)** .... At night they sleep under the two big

(5) ....

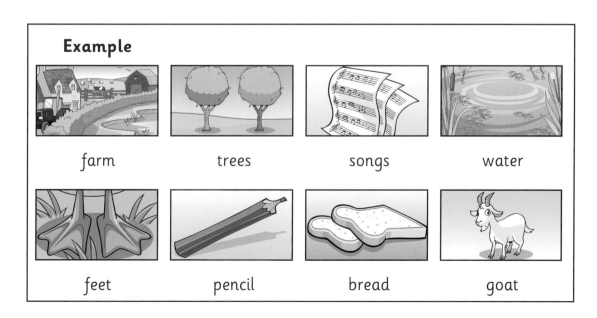

Part 5
– 5 questions –

Look at the pictures and read the questions. Write one-word answers.

Examples

What is behind the park?   a .... *school* ....

How many people are in the red car?   .... *three* ....

Questions

1   Who is angry?   the ....

2   Who is riding a bike?   a ....

3   What is the boy holding?   a ....

4   What colour is the boy's bike?   ....

5   Where are the children riding now?   in the ....

Blank Page

Listening

Part 1
– 5 questions –

Listen and draw lines. There is one example.

Ben   Grace   Mark   Kim

Alice   Hugo   Nick

Part 2
– 5 questions –

**Read the question. Listen and write a name or a number.
There are two examples.**

Examples

What is the name of the girl's brother?   ....Sam....................

How old is the girl's brother?   ....2....................

Questions

1   What is the name of the girl's sister?   ....

2   How old is the girl's sister?   ....

3   What is the name of the girl's
     school?   .... School

4   What is the name of the girl's
     street?   .... Street

5   How many cousins has the girl got?   ....

Part 3
– 5 questions –

Listen and tick (✔) the box. There is one example.

Which fruit can Tom eat now?

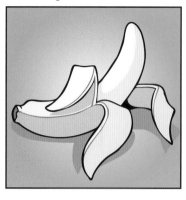  

A ✔   B ☐   C ☐

1   Where is May's tablet?

A ☐   B ☐   C ☐

2   Which sport is Bill playing?

   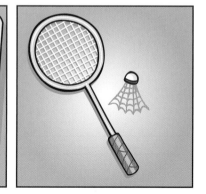

A ☐   B ☐   C ☐

3   What food does Pat want for dinner?

A ☐   B ☐   C ☐

4   What is in the picture in the boy's book?

A ☐   B ☐   C ☐

5   Where is Dan now?

A ☐   B ☐   C ☐

Part 4

– 5 questions –

Listen and colour. There is one example.

Reading and Writing

Part 1
– 5 questions –

Look and read. Put a tick (✔) or a cross (✘) in the box.
There are two examples.

Examples

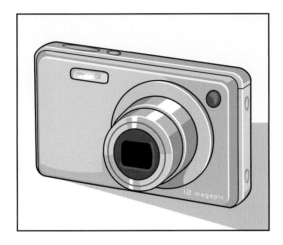

This is a camera.

These are trains.

Questions

1

This is a robot.   ☐

2

This is a bike.　□

3

These are kiwis.　□

4

This is a watch.　□

5

These are cars.　□

Part 2
– 5 questions –

Look and read. Write yes or no.

Examples

There is one teacher in the classroom.   ....yes...............

The door of the classroom is open.   ....no...............

Questions

1   The walls in the classroom are green.   ....

2   The cupboard is under the clock.   ....

3   The girl has got a red pencil on her desk.   ....

4   You can see two posters on the wall.   ....

5   One of the boys is writing on the board.   ....

Part 3
– 5 questions –

Look at the pictures. Look at the letters. Write the words.

Example

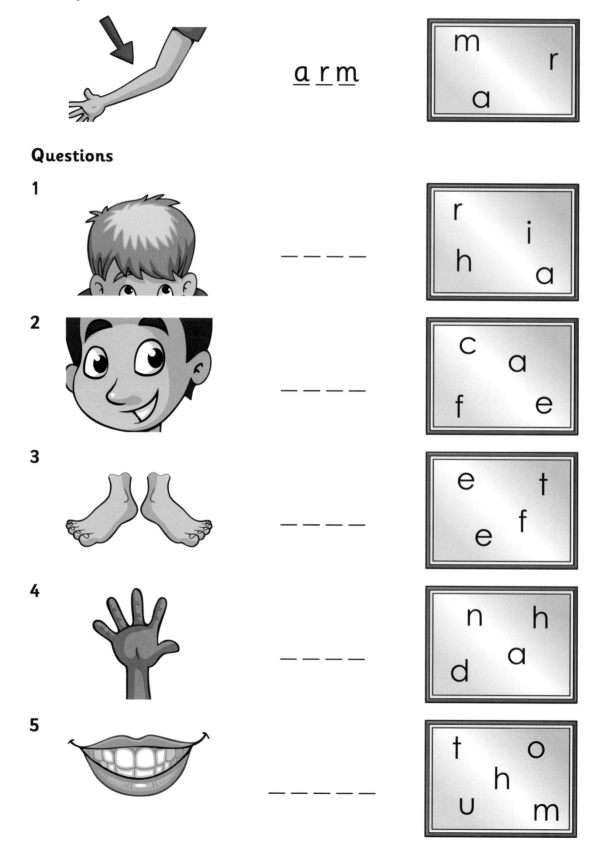

<u>a</u> <u>r</u> <u>m</u>

m   r
a

Questions

1

_ _ _ _

r   i
h   a

2

_ _ _ _

c   a
f   e

3

_ _ _ _

e   t
            f
e

4

_ _ _ _

n   h
    a
d

5

_ _ _ _ _

t   o
    h
u   m

Part 4
– 5 questions –

Read this. Choose a word from the box. Write the correct word next to numbers 1–5. There is one example.

Tom's kitchen

Tom has a big kitchen in his ...house.. . Tom's family sit on

(1) .... and eat their food. Tom likes eating

(2) .... and chips, and his sister likes drinking

(3) .... Tom has some eggs for breakfast and then

he goes to **(4)** .... There are some beautiful

(5) .... from the garden on the kitchen table.

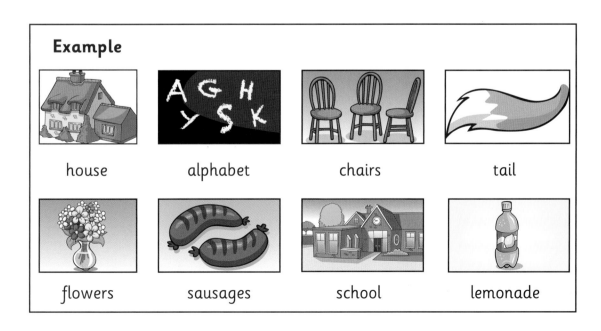

house	alphabet	chairs	tail
flowers	sausages	school	lemonade

Part 5
– 5 questions –

Look at the pictures and read the questions. Write one-word answers.

Examples

Where is the family?   at the ....beach.............

Who is sleeping?   ....Dad.............

Questions

1   How many children are there?   ....

2   Which animal is jumping on the sand?   *the* ....

3   Who is pointing?   ....

4   Who is giving the children ice creams?   ....

5   Where is the dog now?   *in the* ....

Blank Page

Blank Page

Listening

Part 1
– 5 questions –

Listen and draw lines. There is one example.

Pat   Sam   Anna   Dan

Lucy   Nick   Tom

Part 2

– 5 questions –

Read the question. Listen and write a name or a number.
There are two examples.

Examples

What is the boy's name?   Matt

How old is he?   8

Questions

1 How many children are in Matt's class? ....

2 How many pictures are on the wall? ....

3 What is the name of Matt's monster? ....

4 How many eyes has Matt's monster got? ....

5 Who has got a jellyfish monster
in his picture? ....

Part 3
– 5 questions –

Listen and tick (✔) the box. There is one example.

Which sport can they watch on TV now?

A ✔   B ☐   C ☐

1   What does Alex want from the clothes shop?

A ☐   B ☐   C ☐

2   Where is Kim's tablet?

A ☐   B ☐   C ☐

3   What is Ben's favourite food?

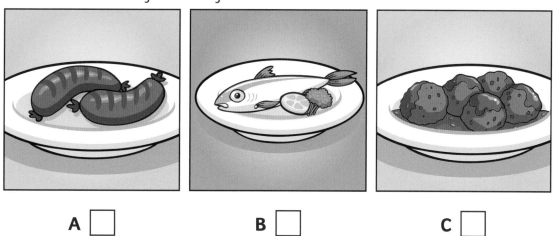

A ☐   B ☐   C ☐

4   Which animal is May's new pet?

A ☐   B ☐   C ☐

5   What is in Dan's school bag?

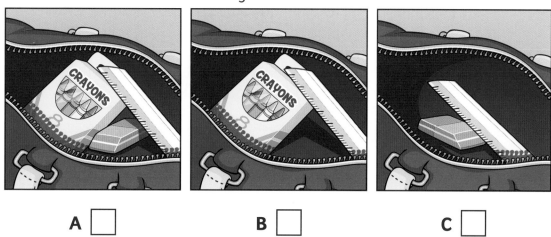

A ☐   B ☐   C ☐

Part 4

– 5 questions –

Listen and colour. There is one example.

Reading and Writing

Part 1
– 5 questions –

Look and read. Put a tick (✔) or a cross (✗) in the box.
There are two examples.

Examples

This is a clock.

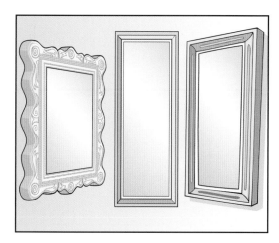

These are mats.

Questions

1

These are burgers.

2

This is a piano. ☐

3

These are crayons. ☐

4

This is a ship. ☐

5

This is a tomato. ☐

Part 2
– 5 questions –

Look and read. Write yes or no.

Examples

There are four monkeys in the trees.	yes
The bird is sitting on the giraffe's head.	no

Questions

1 One of the elephants is in the water. ....

2 A snake is sleeping under a tree. ....

3 Two people are wearing shorts. ....

4 You can see five ducks. ....

5 The crocodile's mouth is closed. ....

Part 3
– 5 questions –

Look at the pictures. Look at the letters. Write the words.

Example

<u>h a t</u>

Questions

1

_ _ _ _

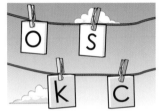

2

_ _ _ _ _

3

_ _ _ _ _

4

_ _ _ _ _

5

_ _ _ _ _ _

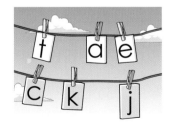

Part 4
– 5 questions –

Read this. Choose a word from the box. Write the correct word next to numbers 1–5. There is one example.

A school

Eva goes to school by ...bus... . She likes her school because it has a big

(1) .... She plays **(2)** .... there

with her friends. Mrs Rice is their **(3)** .... Eva loves

her. In Eva's classroom, there is a **(4)** .... and a big

window. There are lots of **(5)** .... and a board on the

wall. Mrs Rice writes numbers and words on it.

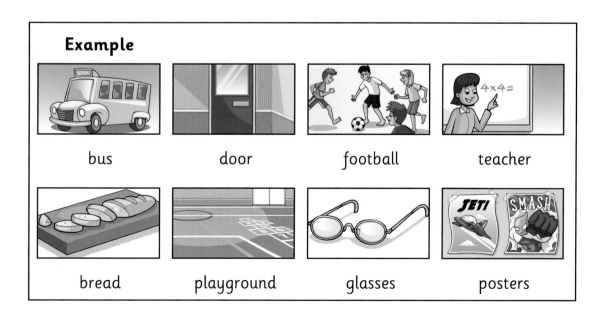

Example

bus   door   football   teacher

bread   playground   glasses   posters

Part 5
– 5 questions –

Look at the pictures and read the questions. Write one-word answers.

Examples

Where are the people?   in the ....Kitchen...........

How many drinks are there
on the table?   ....four...........

Questions

1   What colour are the flowers?   ....

2   What is the girl holding?   a ....

3   Who is singing?   the ....

4   Who is Dad smiling at?   ....

5   What has Mum got?   a ....

Blank Page

Blank Page

OBJECT CARDS

Test 1

Test 1

Test 1

Test 1

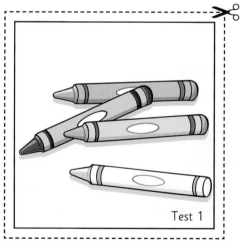

Test 1

Test 1

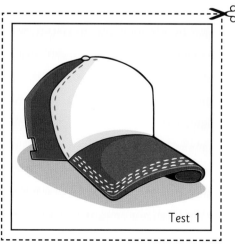

Test 1

Test 1

Blank Page

Speaking

SCENE PICTURE

Blank Page

OBJECT CARDS

Test 2

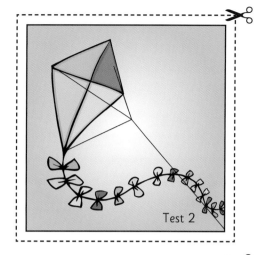

Test 2

Test 2

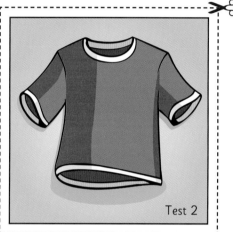

Test 2

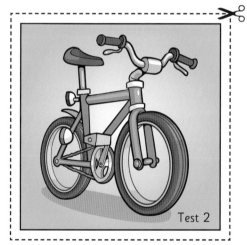

Test 2

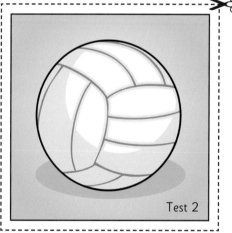

Test 2

Test 2

Test 2

Blank Page

SCENE PICTURE

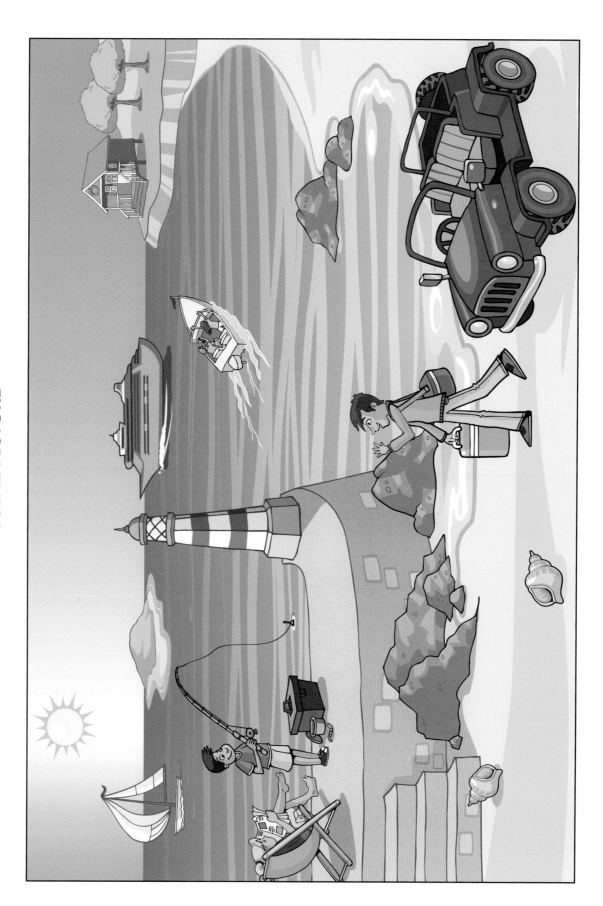

Blank Page

OBJECT CARDS

Test 3

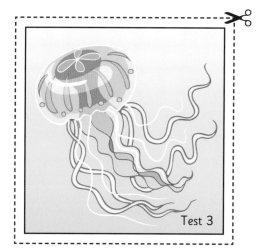

Test 3

Test 3

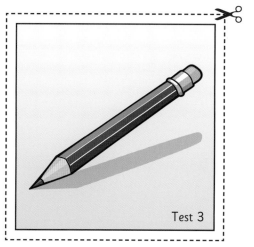

Test 3

Test 3

Test 3

Test 3

Test 3

Blank Page

Blank Page

Blank Page